DISCOVER
UNICORNS
DO YOU BELIEVE?

This series features creatures that excite our minds. They're magic. They're myth. They're mystery. They're also not real. They live in our stories.

T0001977

45th Parallel Press

Published in the United States of America by Cherry Lake Publishing Group
Ann Arbor, Michigan
www.cherrylakepublishing.com

Reading Adviser: Beth Walker Gambro, MS Ed., Reading Consultant, Yorkville, IL
Book Design: Felicia Macheske

Photo Credits: Photo Credits: © Sari ONeal/Shutterstock.com, cover; © Marben/Shutterstock, 1; © Catmando/
Shutterstock, 4; © Olga Vasileva/Shutterstock, 6; © Jannarong Kaewsuwan/Shutterstock, 8; © Natalia
Zhurbina/Shutterstock, 11; © Fer Gregory/Shutterstock, 12; © Kiselev Andrey Valerevich/Shutterstock, 15;
© Renata Sedmakova/Shutterstock, 17; © CoreyFord/iStock, 18; © Elle Arden Images/Shutterstock, 20

Graphic Elements Throughout: © denniro/Shutterstock; © Libellule/Shutterstock; © sociologas/Shutterstock;
© paprika/Shutterstock; © ilolab/Shutterstock; © Bruce Rolff/Shutterstock

Copyright © 2023 by Cherry Lake Publishing
All rights reserved. No part of this book may be reproduced or utilized in any form or by any means
without written permission from the publisher.

45th Parallel Press is an imprint of Cherry Lake Publishing.

Library of Congress Cataloging-in-Publication Data

Names: Loh-Hagan, Virginia, author.
Title: Discover unicorns / Virginia Loh-Hagan.
Description: Ann Arbor, Michigan : Cherry Lake Publishing, [2023] | Series: Magic, Myth, and Mystery Express.
  | Audience: Grades 2-3. | Summary: "What is so magical about a unicorn's horn? Why are unicorn tears so
  special? Books in the Magic, Myth, and Mystery Express series for young readers explore spooky creatures
  that go bump in the night, fill our dreams (or nightmares!), and make us afraid of the dark. Written with a
  high-interest level to appeal to a more mature audience and a lower level of complexity, clear visuals help
  struggling readers along. Considerate text includes fascinating information and wild facts to hold readers'
  interest and support comprehension. Includes table of contents, glossary with simplified pronunciations,
  and index."—Provided by Publisher.
Identifiers: LCCN 2022039297 | ISBN 9781668919637 (hardcover) | ISBN 9781668920657 (paperback)
  | ISBN 9781668921982 (ebook) | ISBN 9781668923313 (pdf)
Subjects: LCSH: Unicorns—Juvenile literature. | Animals, Mythical—Juvenile literature.
Classification: LCC GR830.U6 L635 2023 | DDC 398.24/54—dc23/eng/20221020
LC record available at https://lccn.loc.gov/2022039297

Cherry Lake Publishing would like to acknowledge the work of the Partnership for 21st Century Learning, a
network of Battelle for Kids. Please visit *http://www.battelleforkids.org/networks/p21* for more information.

Printed in the United States of America
Corporate Graphics

Dr. Virginia Loh-Hagan is an author, university professor, former classroom teacher, and curriculum designer. One of her favorite childhood movies was *The Last Unicorn*. She lives in San Diego with her very tall husband and very naughty dogs.

CONTENTS

One Special Horn

Unicorns are magical. They look like horses. They're white. Unicorns have a single horn. It's called an **alicorn**. This is the horn on a unicorn's head. It gives them power.

A spiral shape keeps the alicorn straight.

Have You HEARD?

A Danish throne was made of "unicorn horns." Queen Elizabeth I of England had a "unicorn horn." But they were fakes. The horns were narwhal **tusks**. Tusks are teeth that are like horns. Narwhals are whales.

People talk about unicorn sightings. This has happened for a long time. Sightings are when people see unusual things.

Pegasus is a magical creature. But he has no alicorn. He is not a unicorn.

Did You KNOW?

Lake Superior State University is in Michigan. It gives licenses to hunt unicorns.

Chinese unicorns have deer bodies. They have ox tails. They have horse hooves. They have dragon heads. They have green fish scales.

Persian unicorns are tough. They have rhino bodies. They have lion tails. They have 6 eyes. They have 9 mouths.

There are Eastern unicorns and Western unicorns.

CHAPTER TWO

Magical and Pure

Unicorns are pure. This gives them power. Their alicorns have a lot of power.

Unicorn tears heal wounds. They heal broken hearts.

Almost all parts of the unicorn are powerful.

Unicorns are sensitive. They feel shadows. They walk softly. They don't leave hoofprints. They have sweet voices. They sound like wind chimes.

Alicorns were made into cups. This took away any poisons.

Explained by
SCIENCE

Unicorn horn magic can be explained by **bezoar** stones. Bezoar stones form in the stomachs of some animals. These animals include deer and goats. These stones are made from something the animal eats. They stay in the animal's stomach. People thought bezoars could fight poison.

CHAPTER THREE

Hunted

Unicorns once roamed freely. Then humans saw their magic. Some humans started to hunt unicorns. So unicorns started to hide. They're very hard to find.

Unicorns are difficult animals to hunt. They have many powers.

STAY SAFE!

- Bring a beautiful maiden. Unicorns will get distracted.

- Ask permission to go near unicorns. They can't be tamed.

Unicorns have weaknesses. They like **maidens**. Maidens are pure women. Unicorns go to maidens. They rest near maidens.

Unicorn hunters use maidens as bait.

CHAPTER FOUR

Becoming Pure

Some people think unicorns were the first animals. Unicorns came from the center of Earth. They're perfect.

No one really knows how unicorns came to be.

Know the LINGO!

Buck: jumping into the air with the head low and the back arched

Carbuncle: the gemstone at the bottom of a unicorn's horn

A goddess dreams up a unicorn when she needs one. A unicorn couple gets the baby unicorn. They take care of the baby unicorn. They teach the baby unicorn. They protect the baby unicorn.

Unicorns are too special to be born like other animals.

ORIGINS

Ctesias was an ancient Greek doctor. He traveled. He wrote about new animals. These new animals looked like horses. They had alicorns. More unicorn sightings followed his stories.

REal
WORLD

Liang Xiuzhen lives in China. She's elderly. Some call her the "Unicorn Woman." She has a large skin **tumor** on her head that looks like a horn. A tumor is an unusual growth of tissue on the body.

CONSIDER THIS!

Say What?

Unicorns are magic. How can unicorns fight unicorn hunters?

Think About It!

Some people say unicorns aren't monsters. Some say they are. What do you think?

LEARN MORE

Laskow, Sarah, and Sam Beck. *The Very Short, Entirely True History of Unicorns*. New York: Penguin Workshop, 2019.

Phipps, Selwyn E. *The Magical Unicorn Society: A Brief History of Unicorns*. New York: Feiwel and Friends, 2019.

Seraphini, Temisa, and Sophie Robin. *The Secret Lives of Unicorns*. London; New York: Flying Eye Books, 2019.

Glossary

alicorn (A-luh-korn) a single, spiraled horn coming out of a unicorn's forehead

bezoar (BEE-zohr) stone found in the stomach or intestines of humans and animals

maidens (MAY-duhns) pure women

tumor (TOO-muhr) an unusual growth of tissue on the body

tusks (TUHSKS) long, curved, pointed teeth that are like horns

Index